DATE DUE

AF

SEATTLE SEAHAWKS

by Brian Lester

Published by ABDO Publishing Company, 8000 West 78th Street, Edina, Minnesota 55439. Copyright © 2011 by Abdo Consulting Group, Inc. International copyrights reserved in all countries. No part of this book may be reproduced in any form without written permission from the publisher. SportsZone™ is a trademark and logo of ABDO Publishing Company.

Printed in the United States of America,
North Mankato, Minnesota
062010
092010

Editor: Matt Tustison
Copy Editor: Nicholas Cafarelli
Interior Design and Production: Craig Hinton
Cover Design: Becky Daum

Photo Credits: Ted S. Warren/AP Images, cover, 7, 41; Tom Reed/AP Images, title page; John Froschauer/AP Images, 4; Elise Amendola/AP Images, 8; NFL Photos/AP Images, 10, 13, 14, 22, 25, 42 (top), 42 (middle); AP Images, 16, 18, 21, 42 (bottom); Bill Haber/AP Images, 26; Cheryl Hatch/AP Images, 29; Ben Margot/ AP Images, 30; John Froschauer/AP Images, 33, 43 (top); Elaine Thompson/AP Images, 34, 43 (bottom); Mike Roemer/AP Images, 37, 43 (middle); Miles Kennedy/ AP Images, 38; Greg Trott/AP Images, 44; John Froschauer/AP Images, 47

Library of Congress Cataloging-in-Publication Data
Lester, Brian, 1975-
  Seattle Seahawks / Brian Lester.
     p. cm. — (Inside the NFL)
  Includes index.
  ISBN 978-1-61714-028-0
  1. Seattle Seahawks (Football team)—History—Juvenile literature. I. Title.
  GV956.S4L47 2011
  796.332'6409797772—dc22
                              2010017460

TABLE OF CONTENTS

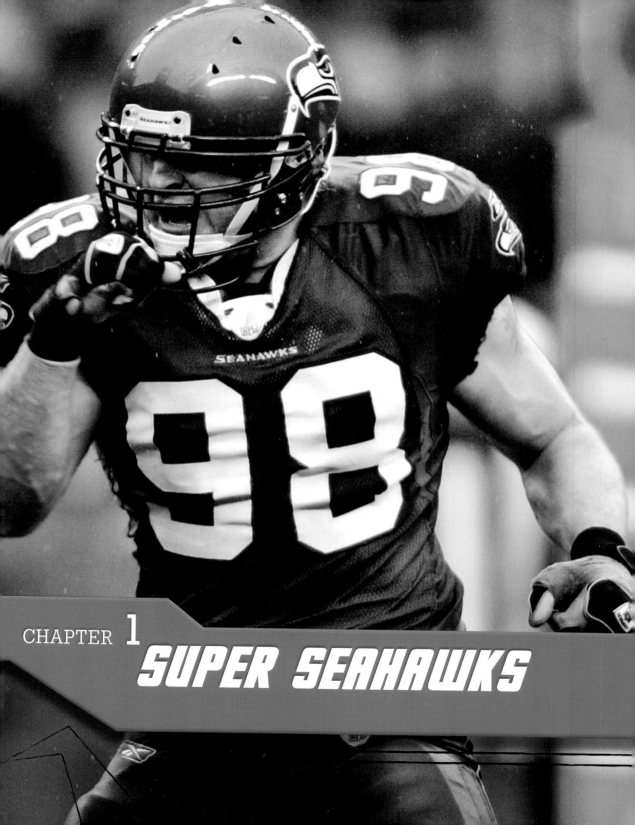

CHAPTER 1

SUPER SEAHAWKS

Fireworks exploded above the scoreboard at Qwest Field in Seattle. A wild crowd roared at jet-engine volume as the clock read all zeroes in the National Football Conference (NFC) Championship Game.

The Seattle Seahawks had defeated the Carolina Panthers 34–14 on January 22, 2006. They were headed to their first Super Bowl. The fans could hardly contain themselves as they took in the moment.

The memories of poor draft decisions and playoff appearances were forgotten on a cold January evening in the Pacific Northwest. Seattle was headed to Super Bowl XL in Detroit, Michigan, to play the Pittsburgh Steelers. "We're not done yet," quarterback Matt Hasselbeck said. "We've got another game to go and win."

SEAHAWKS DEFENSIVE END GRANT WISTROM CELEBRATES DURING SEATTLE'S 34–14 WIN OVER CAROLINA IN THE NFC TITLE GAME ON JANUARY 22, 2006.

BIG HEADACHE

Shaun Alexander was a driving force behind Seattle's success in 2005. He rushed for 1,880 yards and scored 28 touchdowns in the regular season.

But in the Seahawks' first game in the playoffs against the Washington Redskins, the star running back suffered a concussion. Alexander was hit on the side of the head by defensive tackle Cornelius Griffin as he fell to the ground in the first quarter. He was treated by team trainers and left the game. He did not return. But Seattle was able to win 20–10.

Alexander made it back on the field the next week. He played well against the Carolina Panthers and helped Seattle advance to the Super Bowl.

"We have an unbelievable team, an unbelievable group of fans," Alexander said. "Prayer works. I get knocked out and guys step up. One guy goes down and another guy steps up."

The Seahawks dominated the Panthers. Hasselbeck completed 20 of 28 passes for 219 yards and two touchdowns. Shaun Alexander, chosen as the Most Valuable Player (MVP) in the National Football League (NFL) that season, rushed for 132 yards and two touchdowns on 34 carries. Seattle held Carolina to 212 yards and forced four turnovers.

Seahawks coach Mike Holmgren praised the 67,837 fans who attended the game. They had made Qwest Field a tough place to play for the Panthers. As Seattle built momentum during the season, its fans responded. They waved towels and yelled at opposing teams. The Seahawks honored fans as "the 12th Man." Number 12 banners flew atop the Space Needle, from the stadium, and at many office buildings.

SEATTLE COACH MIKE HOLMGREN, BEING INTERVIEWED BY FOX'S TERRY BRADSHAW, RAISES HIS TEAM'S NFC CHAMPIONSHIP TROPHY AFTER ITS WIN OVER CAROLINA.

"They're all coming to Detroit with us. Every one of them," Holmgren said of the fans. "They were great for us all year. Home-field advantage in this place means everything. I think we got people excited about football again here in the Pacific Northwest."

Seattle, which won 11 games in a row in the 2005

NFL'S BEST FANS?

The Seahawks did not lose a home game during the 2005 regular season or postseason. Some of the credit should go to their crazed fans. Seattle was one of only two teams in the NFL to go unbeaten at home during the regular season. Denver was the other team. The Seahawks finished 10–0 at home, counting their two playoff wins. The crowd noise was tough on opposing teams. More false-start penalties by opponents were recorded at Qwest Field than in any other NFL stadium that season.

STEELERS CORNERBACK DESHEA TOWNSEND SACKS SEAHAWKS
QUARTERBACK MATT HASSELBECK IN SUPER BOWL XL. SEATTLE LOST 21–10.

EXPLOSIVE OFFENSE

The Seahawks had the highest-scoring offense in the NFL during their Super Bowl season. They averaged 28.3 points per game during the regular season and were second in total offense with 369.7 yards per game. Seattle kept scoreboard operators busy with 57 touchdowns, the most in the NFL.

regular season after a 2–2 start, led the NFL with 50 quarterback sacks. The team finished with the NFC's best record at 13–3. That earned the Seahawks a bye in the first round of the playoffs. In the next round, Seattle hosted the Washington Redskins and won 20–10. The victory ended a 21-year stretch for the Seahawks without a playoff win.

Unfortunately for the Seahawks, the Super Bowl would not go as well.

Seattle was an underdog against Pittsburgh. The Seahawks fell behind 7–3 by halftime inside Detroit's Ford Field on February 5, 2006. They got as close as 14–10 in the third quarter on Hasselbeck's 16-yard touchdown pass to tight end Jerramy Stevens.

The Steelers' Antwaan Randle El, though, threw a 43-yard touchdown pass to fellow wide receiver Hines Ward on a trick play in the fourth quarter. The score crushed the Seahawks' dream of a championship. Seattle lost 21–10.

"This is a tough pill to swallow," Holmgren said. "We

TOUGH CALL

Luck was not on Seattle's side in Super Bowl XL. With the Seahawks leading 3–0 late in the second quarter, Steelers quarterback Ben Roethlisberger leaped for the end zone. He was met at the goal line by Seattle linebacker D. D. Lewis. It looked as if Lewis stopped Roethlisberger short of the end zone. However, there was not enough evidence in an instant replay to overturn the touchdown ruling on the field. The score gave Pittsburgh a 7–3 lead. The Steelers never looked back.

accomplished a lot this year. While you don't have a great feeling after a game like this, I want them to remember this feeling, so they can build on it."

Seattle would return to the playoffs two more times during the 2000s. But it did not make it back to the Super Bowl. Still, the Super Bowl run during the 2005 season showed how far the franchise had come since its first NFL season in 1976.

CHAPTER 2

REACHING THE "BIG TIME"

Seattle was hungry for a professional football team. On December 5, 1974, the wish of the city's residents came true. The efforts of Lloyd W. Nordstrom and the "Seattle Professional Football" ownership group had paid off. NFL commissioner Pete Rozelle awarded the city a franchise at a news conference in New York.

The new team came with a price tag of $16 million. The money came out of the pockets of some of Seattle's most powerful businessmen, including Nordstrom. He had helped run the major department store chain of the same name. The city had hoped to land a pro football team. So, construction started on the Kingdome in 1972. The Seahawks would begin play in the dome in 1976, their first NFL season. The Tampa Bay Buccaneers would also start playing in 1976 as a new franchise. This gave the league 28 teams.

John Thompson was hired as the Seahawks' general manager. He hired the team's first

SEATTLE QUARTERBACK JIM ZORN SCRAMBLES DURING A GAME IN THE 1976 SEASON, THE SEAHAWKS' FIRST IN THE NFL. THE TEAM WENT 2–12 THAT YEAR.

head coach, Jack Patera. Patera had played in the NFL as a linebacker for three teams. He also had served as an assistant coach with the Los Angeles Rams, the New York Giants, and the Minnesota Vikings. Thompson was very confident in his hiring of Patera. He predicted that the Seahawks would win a Super Bowl within four years.

Sadly, the Seahawks' original owner would never even see the team play a game. Nordstrom died suddenly of a heart attack on January 20, 1976, while vacationing in Mexico. His brother Elmer took over as the owner.

The Seahawks selected 39 players in the NFL Expansion Draft in March 1976. The two new teams, Seattle and Tampa Bay, took turns making picks from lists of players from existing NFL teams. The regular NFL Draft, in which standout college players are selected, was later that spring. The Seahawks chose defensive lineman Steve Niehaus from the University of Notre Dame as their first draft pick. He was taken second overall and became the 1976 NFC Defensive Rookie of the Year.

Seattle discovered two of its greatest players in unconventional ways in 1976. Quarterback Jim Zorn was an undrafted free agent. He made such an impact in his first season that he was named the NFC Offensive Rookie

THE SEAHAWKS' FIRST COACH, JACK PATERA, WATCHES FROM THE SIDELINE DURING A GAME IN 1976. HE WOULD COACH THE TEAM UNTIL 1982.

of the Year. The Houston Oilers drafted wide receiver Steve Largent in 1976. But he was traded before the regular season to the Seahawks for an eighth-round draft pick in 1977. He would become Zorn's favorite target. As of 2010, Largent was the only player in the Pro Football Hall of Fame who played most of his career with Seattle.

HOME SWEET DOME

Work on the Kingdome began in 1972, and its doors opened in 1976. It was officially known as the King County Dome but was referred to as the Seattle Kingdome on national broadcasts. The stadium, considered one of the loudest in the NFL, served as the home of the Seahawks until the 1999 season. It was demolished in 2000.

As the first season approached, the city was buzzing with excitement. However,

QUARTERBACK JIM ZORN AND WIDE RECEIVER STEVE LARGENT TALK DURING SEATTLE'S 13–10 WIN OVER TAMPA BAY ON OCTOBER 17, 1976.

the Seahawks had a team that was mostly made up of rookies and veteran players whom other teams simply did not want. At times, the situation was somewhat chaotic.

"We would have names on our helmets so we would know who was in the huddle with us," said Sam McCullum, a wide receiver on that first team. "It's hard to build camaraderie that way."

The Seahawks went 1–5 in exhibition play in 1976. But the fans did not seem to mind. They could not wait for the regular season to start. A crowd of 58,441 packed into the Kingdome for the opener against the St. Louis Cardinals on September 12, 1976.

"I remember coming out of that tunnel and just the electricity," said Seahawks tight end Ron Howard, who caught seven passes against the Cardinals.

Seattle was knocked around by St. Louis. The Cardinals used a bruising running attack to build a 23–3 lead. With the Seahawks down 30–10 early in the fourth quarter, Zorn hooked up with McCullum on a 72-yard scoring strike. Zorn then rushed 8 yards for another touchdown. The late scores pumped new life into the crowd. Although Seattle ended up losing 30–24, the fans were not disappointed. In fact, many hung around after the game.

"The people were just elated that we were there—not that we had lost or won the game—but just that we were there," McCullum said.

It took six weeks for Seattle to earn its first NFL win. The team picked up a 13–10 road victory on October 17 over fellow new team Tampa Bay. The Seahawks won their

MAKING A NAME FOR HIMSELF

Steve Largent was an All-American at the University of Tulsa but was hardly a top NFL prospect.

The Houston Oilers selected Largent in the fourth round of the 1976 NFL Draft. After four pre-season games, it was expected that he would be released. Instead, Houston traded him to Seattle.

Largent made the most of the opportunity with the Seahawks. He had 54 catches as a rookie. By his third season, he made 71 receptions and reached 1,000 receiving yards for the first time. He would hit the 1,000-yard mark in seven more seasons during his career.

Largent was not the fastest player in the NFL. But he had great hands. He spent 14 seasons with the Seahawks and racked up more than 13,000 receiving yards. Largent was selected to seven Pro Bowls. He was inducted into the Pro Football Hall of Fame in 1995.

THE SEAHAWKS' AUTRY BEAMON, *LEFT*, AND KERRY JUSTIN STOP THE STEELERS' JOHN STALLWORTH IN 1978. SEATTLE FINISHED 9–7 THAT SEASON.

only other game on November 7, when they defeated the Atlanta Falcons 30–13 at the Kingdome. The Seahawks finished their first season with a 2–12 record.

Seattle made a draft mistake in 1977. The Seahawks had the No. 2 overall pick. They traded it away to Dallas for the Cowboys' first-round selection (No. 14 overall) and three second-round choices. Dallas used the

No. 2 pick to draft Tony Dorsett, the Heisman Trophy-winning running back out of the University of Pittsburgh. Dorsett went on to become a Hall of Famer and helped the Cowboys win the Super Bowl his rookie season. The Seahawks took guard Steve August, from the University of Tulsa, with their first-round pick. August and the three second-round choices did not come close to making the impact that Dorsett did in the NFL.

The Seahawks moved from the NFC West to the American Football Conference (AFC) West before the start of the 1977 season. Seattle lost its first four games before topping Tampa Bay 30–23. Two weeks later, Zorn returned from an injury and threw four touchdown passes in a 56–17 rout of the Buffalo Bills at the Kingdome. The Seahawks finished the season 5–9.

In 1978, the Seahawks started 6–6 before stunning the Raiders 17–16 in Oakland. It marked the first time in 13 seasons that any team had defeated Oakland twice in one season. The Seahawks' Efren Herrera made a 46-yard field goal with three seconds left. Largent had 1,168 receiving yards that season and helped Seattle finish with its first winning record, 9–7.

RISING TO THE OCCASION

Quarterback Jim Zorn gave Seattle fans something to cheer about because of his knack for making big plays in big games. In early December in 1978, the Browns were in town and the Seahawks were still in the hunt for a playoff berth. Zorn shredded Cleveland's secondary for 219 passing yards and a touchdown. He completed 15 of his 24 attempts in Seattle's 47–24 win.

Largent earned a spot in the Pro Bowl.

In 1979, the Seahawks lost four of their first five games but recovered nicely for their first *Monday Night Football* contest. Seattle edged host Atlanta 31–28.

The *Monday Night Football* win provided a shot of momentum for the Seahawks. They won five of their final seven games to finish 9–7 again. Patera was named the NFL Coach of the Year. Hope for the future was bright.

CHAPTER 3

BECOMING A CONTENDER

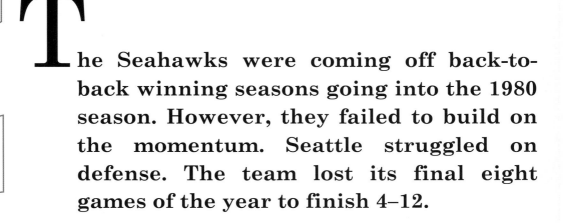

T he Seahawks were coming off back-to-back winning seasons going into the 1980 season. However, they failed to build on the momentum. Seattle struggled on defense. The team lost its final eight games of the year to finish 4–12.

Although Steve Largent racked up 1,224 receiving yards in 1981, he could not save the Seahawks from another losing season. Seattle lost six of its first seven games and finished 6–10.

Jack Patera was fired after the Seahawks lost their first two games of the 1982 season. A players' strike wiped out seven games over the next two months. When the NFL returned to action, Seattle had a new coach. Director of football operations Mike McCormack filled in on a temporary basis. The Seahawks finished with a 4–5 record. McCormack returned to the front office after the season as president and general manager.

QUARTERBACK DAVE KRIEG, SHOWN IN 1989, HELPED THE SEAHAWKS MAKE THE PLAYOFFS FOUR TIMES IN THE 1980s.

SEIZING AN OPPORTUNITY

Dave Krieg did not come to the NFL with much hype. He had been the seventh-string quarterback at one point at tiny Milton College in Wisconsin. Milton College, in fact, no longer exists.

At Milton, he was given a chance to play in the fourth game of his freshman season. Three of his four completions went for touchdowns. He was named the starter for the rest of the season. Krieg's head coach was so impressed as Krieg's career went on that he wrote a letter to the Seahawks and sent game film to the team.

Krieg earned a tryout with the Seahawks after college and made the team in 1980. He would play 12 seasons in Seattle, throwing for 195 touchdowns with just 148 interceptions. Krieg was selected to three Pro Bowls, all while he was a Seahawk. He played 19 seasons overall in the NFL with six teams.

The team welcomed new coach Chuck Knox in 1983. Knox had coached the Los Angeles Rams and the Buffalo Bills. He turned Seattle into a contender.

A change took place at quarterback as well. The popular Jim Zorn would be replaced by Dave Krieg midway through the season. A thrilling 51–48 overtime win over the Kansas City Chiefs in the Kingdome improved the Seahawks to 7–6. Seattle finished 9–7, clinching its first playoff berth in team history with a 24–6 win over the New England Patriots in the regular season's last game.

Krieg, the lowest-paid quarterback in the NFL in 1983, threw for more than 2,000 yards. The playoffs were a chance for him to show his talent. "I think I'm on the threshold of proving myself in this league," Krieg said.

CURT WARNER SCORES THE GO-AHEAD TOUCHDOWN ON A 2-YARD RUN IN SEATTLE'S 27–20 PLAYOFF WIN OVER MIAMI ON DECEMBER 30, 1983.

Indeed, Krieg proved himself in his postseason debut, a wild-card game against the Denver Broncos. In a Christmas Eve showdown against Denver and quarterback John Elway at the Kingdome, Krieg threw for three touchdowns. The Seahawks smashed the Broncos 31–7.

A trip to the Orange Bowl for a divisional-round game against quarterback Dan Marino and the Miami Dolphins was next for the Seahawks. The Dolphins

REMARKABLE ROOKIE SEASON

Curt Warner did not need much time to excel with the Seahawks. Fresh off a senior season at Penn State University in which he led the Nittany Lions to a national title, Warner continued his strong play as a rookie in the NFL. He was the No. 3 overall pick in the 1983 NFL Draft. As a rookie, he ran for 1,449 yards and scored 14 touchdowns (13 rushing, one receiving). His stellar season helped the Seahawks march into the playoffs for the first time in team history.

CHUCK KNOX, SHOWN IN 1984, COACHED THE SEAHAWKS FROM 1983 TO 1991. HE LED THEM TO FOUR PLAYOFF APPEARANCES.

went 12–4 in the regular season and were the defending AFC champions.

With 3:43 remaining in the game, it seemed as if Miami was in control. Seattle trailed 20–17 but refused to give up. Krieg ignited a rally with passes of 16 and 40 yards to Largent. Then rookie running back Curt Warner plunged 2 yards for a touchdown and a 24–20 Seahawks advantage.

Seattle forced Fulton Walker to fumble the ensuing kickoff and recovered the ball. A field goal finished off the 27–20 victory and catapulted the Seahawks into the AFC Championship Game against the Los Angeles Raiders.

"When we came down here, nobody gave us a chance," Knox said. "I can't tell you how proud I am of this team."

The Seahawks would fall short of a trip to the Super Bowl a week later, losing to the Raiders 30–14 on the road. Los Angeles went on to win the Super Bowl. But Seattle had a season it could build on.

And build on it the Seahawks did. They rode the momentum to 12 wins in their first 14 games in the 1984 season. Seattle was successful despite the fact that it lost Warner for the season. He injured his knee in the opening game. Krieg made up the difference. He threw for 3,671 yards and a career-high 32 touchdowns. Seattle's offense was no longer "Ground Chuck," named after the coach's insistence on running the ball often. It was now "Air Knox."

Seattle lost to visiting Denver 31–14 in the regular-season finale and finished with a 12–4 record. The Broncos won the

THEY SAID IT

The 1983 divisional playoff game between Seattle and Miami featured two very different quarterbacks. Dan Marino was a young but established star for the Dolphins. The Seahawks' Dave Krieg, meanwhile, was far from being considered one of the NFL's top quarterbacks. The day before the game, Washington Post sportswriter Michael Wilbon compared the lifestyles of the quarterbacks. "Marino drives to work every morning in a new gold Corvette that matches his hair and arm. Krieg, signed as a free agent, comes in a Pinto."

AFC West. The Seahawks had to settle for a wild-card berth in the postseason.

In their playoff opener, the Seahawks faced the Raiders in a rematch. Seattle forced three turnovers as it beat Los Angeles 13–7 in the Kingdome. A week later, the season would end. Seattle faced Miami again and lost 31–10 on the road.

In the 1985 NFL Draft, Seattle did not have a pick until late in the second round, fifty-third overall. Still, the Seahawks had a chance to select future standouts in the late rounds. But they passed on options such as wide receiver Andre Reed, running back Herschel Walker, and tight end Jay Novacek.

At the time, Walker, who had starred at the University of Georgia, was playing in the United States Football League (USFL). It was a rival league to the NFL. Dallas smartly drafted him, thinking that the USFL would go out of business, which it did. The Seahawks would take six players who combined to play just six games in Seattle. The 1985 season was not all that spectacular either. The Seahawks went 8–8.

Seattle did not make the playoffs in 1986, despite finishing 10–6. A year later, the Seahawks won the right to take linebacker Brian Bosworth, a former star at the University of Oklahoma, in the NFL Supplemental Draft. The supplemental draft is held to accommodate players who do not enter the regular draft.

Seattle went 9–6 in a strike-shortened 1987 season and returned to the playoffs. The trip did not last long, though. The Seahawks lost 23–20 at Houston in overtime.

Bosworth, meanwhile, had a fairly good rookie season.

A SAVIOR IN SEATTLE

Chuck Knox took over as coach in Seattle at a time when the city's excitement for the team was dying down. The fans were tired of the team being average and wanted to see a winner on the field. Knox delivered. He led the Seahawks into the playoffs during his first season and almost guided them to the Super Bowl. Knox won 83 games, including three in the playoffs, in his time as Seahawks coach, from 1983 to 1991.

LINEBACKER BRIAN BOSWORTH WAS A UNIVERSITY OF OKLAHOMA STAR BEFORE THE SEAHAWKS DRAFTED HIM. HE PLAYED FOR SEATTLE FROM 1987 TO 1989.

However, he was forced to retire two years later because of a shoulder injury.

Krieg separated his shoulder early in the 1988 season. The team struggled while Krieg was out. When he returned, Seattle finished strongly and captured its first AFC West title.

A playoff run was not in the cards, however. The host Cincinnati Bengals beat the Seahawks 21–13 in the divisional round. It would be the last postseason appearance for Seattle for a decade. The Seahawks went 7–9 in 1989 to close out the 1980s.

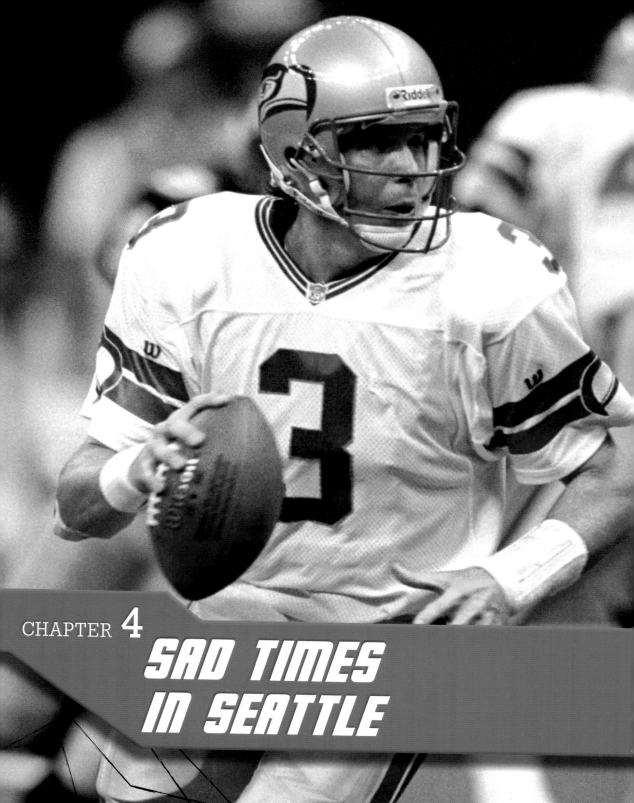

CHAPTER 4

SAD TIMES
IN SEATTLE

Seattle finished a respectable 9–7 in 1990. But it missed out on a trip to the playoffs. There seemed to be hope in 1991 when the team chose quarterback Dan McGwire with the sixteenth pick in the NFL Draft.

McGwire, a younger brother of former major league baseball slugger Mark McGwire, was supposed to be the team's quarterback of the future. However, the ex-San Diego State standout spent most of his rookie season on the sideline. The Seahawks went 7–9, and Chuck Knox resigned as coach after the season.

Tom Flores, who led the Raiders to a pair of Super Bowl championships, was named the new coach.

Quarterback Dave Krieg was no longer with the team either. Seattle had let him leave as a free agent. He signed with division rival Kansas City.

QUARTERBACK RICK MIRER COULD NOT LEAD THE SEAHAWKS TO A WINNING RECORD IN HIS TIME WITH THEM, FROM 1993 TO 1996.

Fans expected to see McGwire play quarterback in 1992. But McGwire lost the starting job to Stan Gelbaugh in the preseason. McGwire played in two games that year and threw three interceptions. He failed to throw a touchdown pass.

McGwire was just one of the problems for the Seahawks. They scored only 140 points during a miserable 2–14 season.

One bright spot was defensive tackle Cortez Kennedy, a rising star. He was in his third season in 1992 and had 14 sacks. He was named the league's Defensive Player of the Year.

There was hope again in 1993 as Seattle gave up on McGwire and drafted Notre Dame quarterback Rick Mirer with the second pick overall. Mirer drew comparisons to San Francisco 49ers legend Joe Montana. Mirer was unable to guide the Seahawks to a winning season. Seattle went 6–10. But Mirer was named the AFC Rookie of the Year.

It was downhill from there. Mirer struggled along with the rest of his team. Seattle never won more than eight games in a season between 1994 and 1996. After a 7–9 season in 1996, the Seahawks released Mirer.

"I think you have people that want to criticize and there's plenty to write about, but overall

DEFENSIVE TACKLE CORTEZ KENNEDY WAS A STANDOUT FOR THE SEAHAWKS IN THE 1990s. HE MADE THE PRO BOWL EIGHT TIMES DURING THAT DECADE.

I think I've been dealt a pretty rough hand," Mirer said. "The first stretch in Seattle I felt we were getting better, things were moving in the right direction. But the roof caved in on us."

Veteran NFL quarterback Warren Moon was a former standout at the University of Washington in Seattle. Moon

NOT THE NEXT MONTANA

Rick Mirer was a standout quarterback at the University of Notre Dame, just like San Francisco star Joe Montana, but the similarities ended there. Mirer played eight seasons in the NFL. Four of those years were spent in Seattle. His most successful season with the Seahawks was in 1993, when he was named the AFC Rookie of the Year. Mirer threw for 2,833 yards and 12 touchdowns with 17 interceptions that season.

QUARTERBACK JON KITNA SIGNED WITH SEATTLE IN 1997 AS AN UNDRAFTED FREE AGENT. TWO YEARS LATER, HE LED THE SEAHAWKS TO THE PLAYOFFS.

was called upon to revive the Seahawks in 1997. He passed for 3,678 yards and 25 touchdowns in his first season in Seattle. But a four-game losing streak near the end of the season left the team at 8–8 and without a play-off berth.

Paul Allen, cofounder of the Microsoft computer corporation, bought the team before the 1997 season. He was eager to make changes. Before the start of the 1998 season, he gave coach Dennis Erickson an ultimatum to either make the playoffs or lose his job.

The Seahawks seemed to be on the right track when they won their first three games. Moon was injured, though, and Seattle turned to backup quarterback

Jon Kitna. Moon returned, and with the Seahawks at 6–6, the team needed a big road win over the New York Jets to keep its playoff hopes alive.

Seattle did not catch a break. The Seahawks fell 32–31 to the Jets. The difference in the game was a questionable late touchdown by New York quarterback Vinny Testaverde. He dove for the end zone, and the play was ruled a touchdown. Replays showed that Testaverde did not have the ball in his hands when he crossed the goal line. The ruling held up, however, and the Jets won.

Seattle went 8–8. Erickson was fired. Mike Holmgren, who had coached the 1996 Green Bay Packers to a Super Bowl title, was brought in to handle the general manager and head coaching duties for the Seahawks in 1999.

DON'T STOP BELIEVING

Jon Kitna probably had no business being an NFL quarterback. He was not recruited by a major college program coming out of high school and even had to walk on at Central Washington University.

But Kitna is a prime example of what hard work and a will to overcome odds can do for a person. He made Seattle's roster as an undrafted free agent and served as a backup in 1997 and 1998. He worked his way into a starting role when Mike Holmgren arrived as coach and general manager in 1999.

Kitna played four seasons with the Seahawks and started 33 games for them. His finest season with Seattle was in 1999. That year, he threw for 23 touchdowns against 16 interceptions and passed for 3,346 yards. He would go on to enjoy some successful seasons with the Cincinnati Bengals (2001–05) and the Detroit Lions (2006–08).

"Now it's my job to come in here and do everything in my power to get the Seahawks to the Super Bowl," Holmgren said at his first news conference.

Seattle fed off Holmgren's enthusiasm. Kitna had a breakout season. He threw for more than 3,000 yards. He helped the Seahawks win eight of their first 10 games. He also won the respect of his teammates.

"He is like steel," running back Ricky Watters said. "He's really focused. He's really detailed in his work, one of the last to come out of meeting rooms."

The Seahawks struggled near the end of the season and lost five of their final six games. They still managed to win the AFC West and played host to Miami in the first round of the playoffs.

"I'm really excited for the whole franchise and everybody to be able to go to the playoffs," Watters said. "But when you lose five of the last six [games], there's got to be a bad taste in everybody's mouth."

The Seahawks were unable to wash out that bad taste in the postseason. Quarterback Dan Marino haunted the team again. He led the Dolphins on a game-winning touchdown drive with five minutes remaining to give Miami a 20–17 win in the last game ever in the Kingdome.

The misery-filled 1990s had come to a close. Despite the tough ending, there was a glimmer of hope for the future.

MIKE HOLMGREN BROUGHT SEATTLE HOPE WHEN HE WAS HIRED AS COACH AND GENERAL MANAGER IN 1999. HE HAD COACHED GREEN BAY TO AN NFL TITLE.

CHAPTER 5

RISING BACK UP

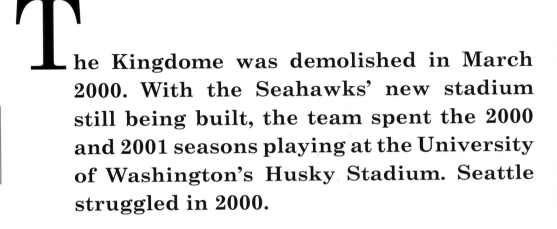

T he Kingdome was demolished in March 2000. With the Seahawks' new stadium still being built, the team spent the 2000 and 2001 seasons playing at the University of Washington's Husky Stadium. Seattle struggled in 2000.

The team started 2–7. The fans no longer loved quarterback Jon Kitna. The Seahawks finished 6–10. Kitna was released. Seattle acquired quarterback Matt Hasselbeck on March 2, 2001. The Seahawks traded their first- and third-round draft picks in 2001 to the Packers for Hasselbeck and Green Bay's first-round pick. Hasselbeck had been drafted by Green Bay in 1998, when Seahawks coach Mike Holmgren was the Packers' coach.

The Seahawks struggled in 2001 with Hasselbeck, though. They signed Trent Dilfer to provide support. Dilfer had been

RUNNING BACK SHAUN ALEXANDER WAS A BIG REASON FOR THE SEAHAWKS' SUCCESS IN THE 2000s. HE WAS NAMED THE NFL'S MVP FOR THE 2005 SEASON.

the starting quarterback on the Baltimore Ravens' Super Bowl-winning team the previous season. Dilfer won in all four of his starts in 2001 with the Seahawks. Second-year running back Shaun Alexander also began to emerge.

In a Sunday night game in November against the Oakland Raiders, Alexander rushed for 266 yards in a 34–27 win. Seattle finished 9–7 but did not make the playoffs.

The 2001 season was the last time Seattle played in the AFC. The NFL made divisional changes before the start of the 2002 season with the addition of a thirty-second team, the expansion Houston Texans. The Seahawks ended up in the NFC West Division.

There was excitement in the air as the Seahawks prepared to play their first season at their new home field, Seahawks Stadium. Seattle faced the Indianapolis Colts in the first exhibition game at the new stadium and lost 28–10. The Seahawks also lost Dilfer to an injury. He sprained his knee in the second quarter.

The bad luck was a sign of things to come in 2002. Seattle lost its first regular-season game at home as well, falling 24–13 to the Arizona Cardinals. The Seahawks were 1–5 in their first six games. Dilfer injured his foot in the team's seventh game, against the Dallas Cowboys. Hasselbeck was called into action and led Seattle to a 17–14 victory.

Hasselbeck did his best to revive the Seahawks' fading playoff hopes. He threw for more than 3,000 yards. The Seahawks missed the playoffs, however. They went 7–9.

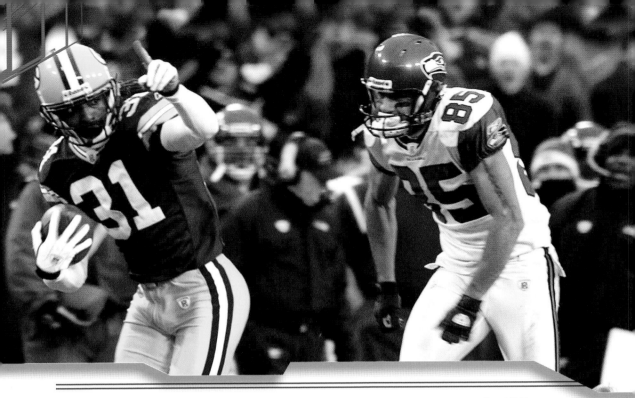

SEATTLE'S ALEX BANNISTER CANNOT CATCH AL HARRIS, WHOSE 52-YARD INTERCEPTION RETURN GAVE GREEN BAY A 33–27 PLAYOFF WIN IN JANUARY 2005.

In 2003, Seattle went unbeaten at home, finished 10–6, and earned a wild-card playoff berth. The Seahawks would travel to Wisconsin to face Green Bay in a playoff opener at chilly Lambeau Field.

Holmgren had coached Green Bay to a Super Bowl title after the 1996 season. Now he would be the Packers' enemy for this game. Seattle rallied in the second half. The game went into overtime tied at 27–27. During the coin flip before overtime, Hasselbeck said Seattle would win the game. His comment was caught by a referee's microphone. He was wrong. Hasselbeck threw an interception that Al Harris grabbed and ran back 52 yards

LINEBACKER LOFA TATUPU RETURNS AN INTERCEPTION 38 YARDS FOR A TOUCHDOWN IN SEATTLE'S 42–0 WIN AT PHILADELPHIA ON DECEMBER 5, 2005.

for the game-winning touchdown in a 33–27 victory for Green Bay.

"What hurts is I had the ball in my hand. I could have done something different, and we don't lose," Hasselbeck said.

In 2004, the Seahawks won the NFC West title with a 9–7 record. In the opening round of the playoffs, the host Seahawks trailed the St. Louis Rams 27–20. Seattle was facing a fourth-and-goal situation with time running out. Hasselbeck hoped to make up for his playoff mistake from the previous year. He threw a pass to Bobby Engram in the end zone. The ball slipped through the wide receiver's hands, though. The Seahawks lost.

Seattle was tired of falling short in the postseason. The Seahawks had not won a playoff game in 20 years. They entered the 2005 season determined to fix that.

Seattle started 9–2 that year. The team did not gain national attention until a *Monday Night Football* showdown with the host Philadelphia Eagles. Andre Dyson and Lofa Tatupu returned interceptions for touchdowns during a 35-point outburst in the first half. The Seahawks won 42–0 for their eighth straight victory.

The Seahawks ended the year with a 13–3 record and home-field advantage throughout the playoffs. Magic was in the air at Qwest Field (the new stadium was renamed in 2004). Wins over Washington and Carolina launched Seattle into the Super Bowl against Pittsburgh. Despite a remarkable playoff run, the Seahawks fell to the Steelers 21–10. They walked away without the ultimate prize, a Super Bowl title.

The Seahawks reached the playoffs again in 2006 after going 9–7. They edged visiting Dallas 21–20 in the wild-card round but lost to host Chicago in overtime in the next round. Robbie Gould nailed a 49-yard field goal to give the Bears a 27–24 victory. After a 10–6 regular season in

BROTHER ACT

Seahawks running back Julius Jones and his brother Thomas made history together during the 2006 season. They became the first brothers to both rush for more than 1,000 yards in the same season. Julius Jones ran for 1,084 yards for Seattle, and Thomas had 1,210 for Chicago.

BACK IN THE NFL

When Pete Carroll was named coach of the Seahawks in January 2010, it was not the first time he had landed an NFL coaching job.

Carroll had coached the New York Jets in 1994 and won only six games. From 1997 until 1999, he was coach of the New England Patriots. He posted a 28–23 record (including 1–2 in playoff games) with that team.

Carroll, known for his youthful energy and enthusiasm, then became a head coach in the college ranks at the University of Southern California. It was a strong fit. Carroll was one of college football's most successful coaches in the 2000s.

He wanted to try coaching in the NFL again, though. He was thankful that the Seahawks had given him another shot in the league. He also spoke in his first news conference about raising the level of expectations in Seattle.

2007, the Seahawks beat visiting Washington 35–14 in the playoffs. The win set up another showdown at Green Bay.

The Seahawks turned two turnovers into touchdowns early on to build a 14–0 lead against the Packers on a snowy afternoon. Green Bay and quarterback Brett Favre bounced back in a big way, though, and won 42–20.

Through the 2009 season, Seattle had not been back to the playoffs since. The Seahawks were just 4–12 in 2008. Holmgren retired from coaching after that season. Seattle was only slightly better in 2009 under new coach Jim Mora Jr., who had the title of Seahawks assistant head coach the previous two seasons. Mora had been Atlanta's head coach from 2004 to 2006 before going to Seattle. The Seahawks finished just

PETE CARROLL ANSWERS QUESTIONS AFTER HE WAS INTRODUCED AS THE SEAHAWKS' COACH AND EXECUTIVE VICE PRESIDENT ON JANUARY 12, 2010.

5–11 under him in 2009. The team fired him in January 2010.

A new era began that same month when former University of Southern California (USC) coach Pete Carroll was hired to coach the Seahawks. At USC, Carroll went 97–17 and won two national titles. The Seahawks' top officials were hopeful that Carroll could restore glory to the once-proud team.

Carroll was given a five-year contract worth $35 million. "I hope we can do things better than it's ever been done around here," Carroll said. "There are extraordinarily high expectations, and I love living in that world."

TIMELINE

1974	Seattle is awarded an NFL franchise. Lloyd W. Nordstrom heads up an ownership group that pays $16 million for the team.
1976	The Seahawks play their first season in the NFL. They finish 2–12.
1978	Seattle posts its first winning season. It finishes 9–7, with two wins against the Oakland Raiders.
1983	Chuck Knox is named the Seahawks' coach in January.
1984	Seattle finishes the 1983 season 9–7 and earns a wild-card playoff spot. After beating the Denver Broncos and the Miami Dolphins, the Seahawks lose to the Los Angeles Raiders in the AFC Championship Game on January 8.
1984	Seattle reaches the playoffs again as a wild card. The Seahawks defeat the Raiders but cannot overcome Dan Marino and the Dolphins in a divisional-round loss on December 29.
1988	The Seahawks win their first division title but cannot use the success to fuel a Super Bowl run. Seattle loses to the Cincinnati Bengals in the divisional round on December 31.
1991	Knox resigns as coach after the season and is replaced by Tom Flores, who also becomes the general manager. Flores had won two Super Bowls while coaching the Raiders.
1994	Flores is fired in late December as coach and general manager after three seasons with the Seahawks. Former University of Miami coach Dennis Erickson is hired as Seattle's coach the next month.

1997	Microsoft cofounder Paul Allen purchases the Seahawks.
1998	Seattle misses out on a playoff berth as it finishes 8–8. Erickson is fired in late December.
1999	Seattle hires former Green Bay Packers coach Mike Holmgren as coach and general manager in January.
2000	The Kingdome is demolished. The Seahawks move into their temporary home at Husky Stadium.
2002	Seattle opens its new stadium, Seahawks Stadium. In 2004, it would be renamed Qwest Field. The Seahawks, who move over to the NFC West from the AFC West, fail to reach the playoffs. They finish with a 7–9 record.
2004	Seattle plays at Green Bay in the playoffs and loses 33–27 on January 4. The game pits Holmgren against his former team. An interception thrown by the Seahawks' Matt Hasselbeck is returned for a touchdown in overtime.
2006	The Seahawks finish the 2005 season with their best record ever, 13–3, and secure home-field advantage in the playoffs. It pays off as the Seahawks defeat the Carolina Panthers 34–14 on January 22 to win their first NFC Championship Game and reach their first Super Bowl. In Super Bowl XL against the Pittsburgh Steelers on February 5, the Seahawks fall behind but get as close as 14–10. Pittsburgh, though, pulls away to win 21–10.
2010	Pete Carroll leaves his job as coach at the University of Southern California to become the Seahawks' coach in January after Jim Mora Jr. is fired the same month. It marks Carroll's third stint as a head coach in the NFL.

QUICK STATS

FRANCHISE HISTORY

1976–

SUPER BOWLS

2005 (XL)

AFC CHAMPIONSHIP GAMES
(1977–2002)

1983

NFC CHAMPIONSHIP GAMES
(1976, 2003–)

2005

DIVISION CHAMPIONSHIPS

1988, 1999, 2004, 2005, 2006, 2007

KEY PLAYERS
(position, seasons with team)

Shaun Alexander (RB, 2000–07)
Dave Brown (DB, 1976–86)
Kenny Easley (S, 1981–87)
Jacob Green (DE, 1980–91)
Matt Hasselbeck (QB, 2001–)
Walter Jones (OT, 1997–2008)
Cortez Kennedy (DT, 1990–2000)
Dave Krieg (QB, 1980–91)
Steve Largent (WR, 1976–89)
Curt Warner (RB, 1983–89)
John L. Williams (FB, 1986–93)
Jim Zorn (QB, 1976–84)

KEY COACHES

Mike Holmgren (1999–2008):
    86–74–0; 4–6 (playoffs)
Chuck Knox (1983–91):
    80–63–0; 3–4 (playoffs)

HOME FIELDS

Qwest Field (2002–)
    Known as Seahawks Stadium
    2002–03
Husky Stadium (2000–01)
Kingdome (1976–99)

* All statistics through 2009 season

QUOTES AND ANECDOTES

"I think he's going to be fine" for the NFC Championship Game, Seahawks coach Mike Holmgren said of running back Shaun Alexander after he suffered a concussion in Seattle's divisional-round victory over the Washington Redskins in the 2005 playoffs. "I think if I had showed him a picture of a truck, he would have said it was a truck—and not a butterfly."

A name-the-team contest for the Seahawks drew 20,365 entries. Here are some of the potential names Seattle could have had when it joined the NFL: Anchovies, Bumbershoots, Clam Guns, Evergreens, Identified Flying Objects, Sockeyes, and Worms. It was determined that the Seahawks was the most suitable name and made the most sense geographically.

The players on the Seahawks in the first few seasons participated together in Bible study, prayer, hospital visits, and offseason charity basketball games. Coach Jack Patera rarely had to worry about discipline problems.

Coach Jack Patera climbed into his car one night. Something did not feel right. He could not tell what until he put the car in gear. The wheels spun, and the car did not move. He realized he had been tricked. "We jacked up the back of his car one night," said Art Kuehn, a former center for the Seahawks. "[Tackle] Nick Bebout and I did it. Then we just sat in the bushes and laughed."

GLOSSARY

berth

A place, spot, or position, such as in the NFL playoffs.

bye

The position of a team or person in a tournament that advances to the next round without playing.

exhibition game

A game, typically played before the official start of the season, that does not factor into the standings.

expansion

In sports, to add a franchise or franchises to a league.

franchise

An entire sports organization, including the players, coaches, and staff.

hall of fame

A place built to honor noteworthy achievements by athletes in their respective sports.

momentum

A continued strong performance based on recent success.

Pacific Northwest

A region of the northwest United States, including Oregon and Washington.

postseason

The period after the end of a regular season in which additional games or playoffs are held, especially to determine a champion.

precise

Exact, as in performance, execution, or amount; accurate or correct.

retire

To officially end one's career.

rookie

A first-year professional athlete.

secondary

The defensive players who line up behind the linebackers to defend the pass and assist with run coverage.

FOR MORE INFORMATION

Further Reading

Cluff, Chris, Paul Moyer, and Dave Wyman. *Then Zorn Said to Largent: The Best Seattle Seahawks Stories Ever Told.* Chicago: Triumph Books, 2008.

Seattle Times. *Super Seahawks: The Story of the Seahawks' Magical Run to the Super Bowl.* Chicago: Triumph Books, 2006.

Turner, Mark Tye. *Notes from a 12 Man: A Truly Biased History of the Seattle Seahawks.* Seattle: Sasquatch Books, 2009.

Web Links

To learn more about the Seattle Seahawks, visit ABDO Publishing Company online at **www.abdopublishing.com**. Web sites about the Seahawks are featured on our Book Links page. These links are routinely monitored and updated to provide the most current information available.

Places to Visit

Pro Football Hall of Fame
2121 George Halas Drive NW
Canton, OH 44708
330-456-8207
www.profootballhof.com
This hall of fame and museum highlights the greatest players and moments in the history of the National Football League. As of 2010, there were six Hall of Famers who had spent at least a part of their careers with the Seahawks. Chief among them was wide receiver Steve Largent.

Qwest Field
800 Occidental Ave. S. Ste 100
Seattle, WA 98134
206-381-7555
www.qwestfield.com
Qwest Field has a capacity of 67,000 and is the home field of the Seahawks. Tours of the stadium are available and last about 90 minutes.

Seattle Seahawks headquarters
11220 NE 53rd St.
Kirkland, WA 98033
425-827-9777
www.seahawks.com
The Seahawks began construction on their new headquarters in the fall of 2006. In 2008, the team began using the facility for its training camp instead of Eastern Washington University.

INDEX

About the Author

Brian Lester is a sportswriter who has spent the past eight years covering the University of Findlay for *The Courier* in Findlay, Ohio. He has won two Associated Press awards in Ohio. He lives with his wife and daughter.